YACHTS UNDER SAIL

The cutter Golliwogg loafs behind the ultimate in parachute spinnakers.

YACHTS
UNDER SAIL

a collection of photographs with foreword by

ALFRED F. LOOMIS

the book designed by
Gordon C. Aymar

•

John de Graff, Inc.   :   Tuckahoe, N.Y. : 1974

To a certain crew

WORTH, BOBBY, SALLY AND HARVEY

Introduction

The older generation of sailors has neglected to let the rest of us in on Alfred Loomis's special genius as a boating writer. Since his death at age seventy-seven in 1968, there has been no ready access to his witty, knowledgeable books about yachts and yachting. Perhaps we are all overly preoccupied with our sport's technical fascinations and too little concerned with its literary heritage. Whatever the reason, this reprinting of Alf Loomis's 1933 photo book—occasioned by his family's discovery of the original glossies in their barn—should introduce this best of all boating writers to younger readers.

I am lucky, among my peers under thirty, to have known Loomis. I spent my adolescent summers afloat near the Long Island Sound mooring of his little cutter *Hotspur,* on whose brass and brightwork he labored as I sailed around her and him in shy, admiring circles. I also read his books. Not all eighteen of them, I admit, since his histories of ocean racing and on the America's Cup, his seven boys' sailing adventure books and his one novel were not in my family library. But I returned summer after summer to his five cruising books, his two yachting yearbooks and—my favorite—*Yachts Under Sail.* One of the many wry captions has since come to mind during every nasty watch on every ocean race I have sailed. It accompanies the photograph of a hard-driven schooner: "The *Bagheera,* running, as usual, for shelter in a race on Lake Michigan. The shelter lay just beyond the finish." There is not a wasted word or (in the recitation) breath in this resigned acceptance of ocean racing's demands.

Alf Loomis was forty-two when he edited this volume. Behind him lay ten yachting and boys' books and a career as a free-lance writer about power boats and automobiles. He was soon to join the staff of *Yachting*, where as "Spun Yarn" he would for thirty-four years fill a column called "Under the Lee of the Longboat" with pointed and humorous thrusts at nautical misadventures. He was a self-taught sailorman, having taken up the sport at age thirty-one while rolling down to Panama in a small yawl. That first sailboat cruise (he had made passages in powerboats) stimulated his first and best cruising book, the light-hearted *Cruise of the Hippocampus*. He caught the ocean racing bug in the mid-twenties, between long cruises, and was eventually to sail as navigator in eleven Fasnet and seventeen Bermuda races. Ocean racing from Honolulu to Buenos Aires to Miami to Bermuda to Cowes was to be his professional world until his death.

So it is not surprising that much of this book focuses on ocean racing. Four years later Loomis would be more scholarly in his definitive history of the sport, *Ocean Racing*, but here summarized in photographs are its joys and agonies—plus something of its history. For the latter compare the photos of *Malabar X*, a full-ended fisherman-type schooner that won the 1932 Bermuda Race, and *Dorade*, a narrow yawl that took Class B in that race, a year after she had won both the Transatlantic and Fasnet races. Malabar was the last successful ocean racer of her type and *Dorade* was the first of hers. Fortunately for posterity, the photographer found the yawl that day with her twenty-three-year-old designer Olin Stephens at her helm, his even younger brother Rod at his left hand.

But you needn't know such details to enjoy this artistic and graceful book. To paraphrase the last of Alf Loomis's captions, "Good reading, sailor. Handsome photos and fine writing to you."

John Rousmaniere
Associate Editor
Yachting
November 15, 1973

F o r e w o r d

This book is an attempt to reproduce pictorially the dramatic action and the intrinsic beauty of the yacht under sail— a photographic song without words. In its inception it was planned as a portrayal of modern yachts of definite classifications, with studies that would prove interesting technically to racing yachtsmen, and with glamorous portraits of swelling canvas that would attract the layman. Traces of the original plan may be seen in the eventual selection of the pictures in the book, but, I am happy to say, only traces.

As the characters in a novel are said to run away with the author, so the photographs, as I unearthed them from the files of professional and amateur photographers, ran away with me. I had known for years of the existence of such striking photographs as Levick's Forties in a Squall and Rosenfeld's miraculous snap of a Sound Interclub with her mast bent almost double, but I had no notion that I would find nearly a hundred pictures that claimed admittance to a collection on the score of sheer photographic merit. Thus the book lost its vague pretensions of being a symposium of modern sailing yachts and became instead a pictorial invitation to the most exhilarating of sports.

Consistency of form or style having been cast to the winds,

a certain criterion of perfection evolved to take its place. If, in running through thousands of yacht photographs, I came across one that made me wish enviously that I had been aboard when the picture was taken, that picture became part of the collection. Similarly, if I found myself mentally exclaiming, "I'm glad I wasn't there," the picture evoking that weak sentiment was also included. Into the latter category fell, at first, the wrecks and dismastings that will be seen at the end of the book; yet I learned, surprisingly enough, that after I had inspected these a few times most of them transferred themselves into the affirmative classification. I'd like to be aboard some day when a mast lets go—not aboard my own boat, thank you, but aboard a friend's to see how it happens and to hear what the responsible person says. So, everything considered, the most logical explanation that I can advance for the collection as it stands is that each picture appealed to me as portraying one or more of the varied fascinations of yachting.

*   *   *   *

At this juncture, however, I feel impelled to enter a blanket apology to those readers who on completing the book say, "What! No picture of the So-and-So?" These absentee pictures, as I belatedly realize, are as numerous as yachtsmen and the yachts they cherish. Every yacht owner has one, enlarged, printed in sepia, and hanging on the wall. To each owner the picture is the essence of marine photography and the quintessence of spread canvas and foaming sea. Heaven is my witness that I assaulted friends, acquaintances, and strangers with written and spoken appeals for such sine qua nons. To every offended reader I may only plead that my commission as compiler of a book of photographs did not include the right of search of private homes.

* * * *

Mention of the reader necessitates a short aside to the layman who may think the word misused. The academic question is, "Does the word 'reader' apply to one who looks at a book of pictures?" The answer is, "Yes, when the pictures are those of yachts under sail." As proof I beg to call attention to a miniature on this page, showing three sailors looking aloft. That's not all it shows to the discerning yachtsman. It tells the story of an ocean-racing schooner off the wind on the port tack, the working jib boused down on the bowsprit and the balloon jib (which can't be seen) pulling like a train of cars. It shows the maintopmast balloon staysail spread out on the cabin house ready for instant use and three members of the crew gathered at the mainmast to discuss the racing situation.

The man with the pipe and little else says, "The fisherman is certainly paying its way and I think the golliwobbler (slang for maintopmast balloon staysail) would give us another knot."

The overdressed gentleman who rests his hand against the Marconi mast shows signs of being a bit skeptical. "Mmmmm,"

he says. "I wouldn't say the wind had faired enough quite yet. Look how the luff of the fisherman lifts just a leetle when her bow drops down in the trough. I'd wait a bit if you asked me."

The third man, whom I take to be the navigator, from his tense, strained attitude, says, "God, man, we're racing. Knock her off a point and set the golliwobbler and it will fill and start us footing. The only thing is, don't stand here all day jawing."

So there's quite a bit of reading to that one small picture, and not a hundredth part as much cursing as a private movie-tone reproduction of this book would bring out in certain others. Take also the striking picture of the ketch Marilen in the body of the book. What does the informed reader see in that? Probably twice as much as I do, but including the telling fact that the owner has sheeted her flat and then sailed her full so that the wind will knock her down, roll her side out, and make her look as if she were logging fifteen. The mast-head pennants, streaming out abeam, tell that little story.

On the other hand the yachtsman-reader will observe with delight and appreciation the picture showing the stern of the cup defender Enterprise. She also is sheeted flat, not because there's a photographer in the offing, but because that's the way she sails when jammed hard on the wind.

To find one more instance of the readability—I might almost say the verbosity—of the pictures, search through the book until you come to the two of the Valiant with her mast inverted. In the lower view there's a man standing aft with his arms akimbo, and what's he saying to the sad sea waves? Just this: "Exactly what I could have told Starling if he'd asked me. Spending all that money on a trick duralumin mast only to have it pop out with the first catspaw. Hell!"

*   *   *   *

Apropos of the mishap to the Valiant I asked the photographer, as many readers of the book will no doubt ask themselves, why a shot was not taken in the instant of the mast's collapse. The tall built-up spar was frankly an experiment and many doubts of its strength had been expressed. Why, then, wasn't the picture-taker ready when the expected happened? He was ready. Not only that, but he was armed with a premonition that had made him follow the Valiant for half an hour with camera leveled and shutter set. And at the climactic instant a motor boat got in the way and spoiled the view. "I had my choice," said Rosenfeld, sadly, "of missing the shot or of ramming the motor boat and sinking it. It seemed wiser not to ram the motor boat." He should be decorated for stoic fortitude in the face of virtuous temptation.

*   *   *   *

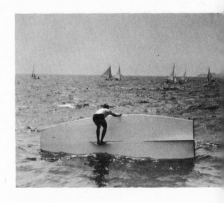

In my selection of these photographs I have imposed two arbitrary limitations having nothing to do with the excellence of the pictures themselves. The first of these is geographical, the boats included being those that would show American

colors if it were customary for yachts under sail to fly the national ensign. The other restriction is chronological, the collection comprising a cross section of yachting since the war. In both limitations I have strayed away from the paths of consistency—most flagrantly in the example of the famous cutter Jolie Brise. There are other exceptions as in the cases of the Irish Shamrock V, the Canadian Quest, and the Vanitie— American in every particular, but under her 1914 rig. I have my ingenious excuses for these departures from plan, but in the inclusion of the Jolie Brise, a British boat, French built, photographed in English waters, I have only one excuse— namely, that without her the book would not be complete.

Jolie Brise it was that in 1926 sauntered (if I may use the word) into Larchmont after a 48-day passage from England to take part in our five-day ocean race to Bermuda. By the staunchness of her construction and the modesty of her intrepid owner she endeared herself to local yachtsmen from the day of her unheralded entrance upon the American scene. The Bermuda race sailed, she cruised back to England where in the course of years she frequently engaged in friendly competition against Americans who had been induced, largely by the force of her example, to cross the Atlantic and race abroad. In 1932, under different but no less gallant ownership, she returned to America to contest once more for the Bermuda cup, the premier trophy of our ocean racing yachtsmen.

She started the race and in the blackness of the first night at sea Robert Somerset, her owner, looked astern and saw the red glare of a burning yacht. He put back and despite a dirty chop and strong wind took off the crew of the burning Adriana. One man missed his footing in the jump for safety and was lost. Without the Jolie Brise ten others would have shared his fate. In every gallery of fame the Brise belongs.

*   *   *   *

We have our other celebrities, including the Nina, winner of virtually every long-distance trophy until the Dorade succeeded her, and the Dorade herself, holder of the trans-Atlantic record in the phenomenal time (for so small a boat) of sixteen days and twelve hours. We have also the three-masted schooner Atlantic which in 1905 established the all-time yacht record for a passage between America and England of twelve days and four hours, and is still going strong. Here also we see the Highland Light and the Wander Bird, the latter a big ex-pilot boat which each summer makes her trans-oceanic voyage, and for contrast the diminutive 18-foot Elaine which recently sailed with one man from Australia to America. We have, as previously intimated, the most famous of all yachts, the Shamrock and the Enterprise.

Although not all types of afternoon racing boats are included we have Frostbite Dinghies, Stars, Sixes, Eights, Twelves, and many others; and I confess to no small amount of enthusiasm in saying that whether they are on the wind or off their pictures induce an overwhelming urge to go afloat again.

*   *   *

Another apology impends. A majority of the intimate views of life aboard sailing yachts prove to have been taken by myself—not because my photographs of this genre were better than others, but because, having been navigator of different craft in ocean contests I have generally been the one soul aboard who had nothing to do but sleep or take pictures.

With this small exception on the plane of personal embarrassment, most of the credit for the excellence of the pictures goes to the photographers themselves, whose names and achievements will be found listed on a succeeding page. The balance of the credit rightly belongs with Gordon Aymar who laid out the original photographs with such an eye for the beautiful and the dramatic that I came within an ace of piously entitling the book, "God! What Pictures!"

A. F. L.

Frostbiting, the popular pastime of racing dinghies throughout the northern winter, is not always accompanied by gales of wintry strength. Occasionally the hard-bitten sailors drift companionably around the course, incurring no overwhelming risk of drowning.

The 6-meters Lucie, Nancy and Jill tuning up for racing in the Solent.

The 8-meter Quest, 1930 challenger for the Canada's cup, sailing off Rochester, N. Y. The cup, long in American possession, was successfully defended by the Thisbe.

Six-meters about to start in a breeze of wind. Number 8 has luffed K 12 across the line, 3 has come into stays ro play for time, and K 20, bearing off, is praying that the gun will fire soon. Such craft, designed exclusively for racing and perfect for the purpose, seem small to cruising yachtsmen.

Such a cruising boat as the 18-foot Elaine seems small to any sailor. Yet she is big enough and sturdy enough to have permitted Fred Rebell, her owner, to sail her single-handed from Sydney, N. S. W., to Los Angeles. As he was not racing he spent a year on the passage, logging about 9000 miles.

An afternoon's racing from an unusual point of view. Anchored off Rye, the Mother Goose, doing duty as committee boat, starts the Victory class across the line. Letters indicate the other classes racing, and a committee member is seen about to haul down the signal.

Fitting out dinghies that have been brought by car and boat to a midwinter rendezvous, the picture proving that it isn't only the racing that makes sailing popular. It's the opportunity to compare and criticise and to wear any old garment that warms and pleases.

Action and determination aboard the Thistle of the Wee Scot class. Crew: "Wait a minute—I'll tell 'em." Skipper: "Let your weather jib sheet run and we'll get away from here." Crew: "Give me some time to blow the man down."

Class E Inland Lakes scow off before the wind at Seaside, Park, N. J. When the right conditions prevail, these flat-bottomed boats sometimes plane on the surface at speeds estimated between twelve and fif- tween miles an hour.

An Atlantic once asserted her right to luff as she started a race. The committee boat marked the weather end of the line, and a few of the Atlantics marked it. Nobody minded, as it was all done in a moment of inattention.

Twenty - one - foot Fish class
sloops racing for the Lipton cup,
most important trophy of the
Gulf Coast yachtsmen. Such
races are sailed annually at Bi-
loxi, Houston, Mobile, New Or-
leans, Pensacola, St. Petersburg,
or Sarasota.

The Flying Cloud, a modified dugout canoe under such a cloud of canvas as is only seen in Chesapeake Bay. Note the live ballast, ready to lay out along the hiking boards.

Something more closely resembling real sailing weather.
The big F class schooner Pleione, off Sakonnet, R. I., dusting
off a few whitecaps on a New York Yacht Club cruise.

Calm weather on Lake Ontario.
It has blown before and perhaps it will one day blow again,
but either of these competitors
in a Toronto trophy race could
do with a breath of air at the
fateful moment of approaching
the finish line. Swearing won't
help; patience does it.

Among the smallest in size, the Stars comprise the world's largest fleet of racing boats. With a required crew of two the skipper steers with hands or feet, while the other handles sail and engages in ballastic acrobatics. Here a fleet of Stars is racing off San Pedro.

Larchmont week, just before the crash—the financial crash.
Here were Fishes, Interclubs, Victories, Stars, Atlantics
and many others in a soft spot.

Vanitie, 1920 cup defense candidate, in her 1914 gaff-headed rig. Rerigged often, she has been a schooner and is now again a sloop. In whatever raiment this Gardner-designed yacht is beautiful.

Tenth of the line of Malabar, John Alden's enduring contribution to cruising yacht design. Under his captaincy in ocean racing in recent years Alden schooners have won with traditional regularity.

Nina, famed winner of the 1928 race to Spain. Combining the reaching qualities of a schooner off the wind and a cutter's weatherly ability when close-hauled, she has been invincible in many contests.

Ketch Seven Bells doing
nothing in particular.

The schooner Wiletie going
somewhere very fast.

A camera study of sails and rigging.
Aloft in the Migrant, a three-masted
ocean-going schooner.

Schooner Atlantic short-tacking off the coast of Spain in the race of '28.

Loosing her top-sails as she settles to a long board on the port tack.

Looking down on deck of the Burgess-designed Enterprise
and on her boat-shaped main boom, so fitted with thwart-
ship tracks and slides that the foot of its sail may assume
a curve most conducive to a speedy flow of air.

Not the Flying Dutchman, but the Marilen, a San Franciscan ketch going through her paces before the camera's eye, sails trimmed flat and wind abeam. It is the land and not a colossal sea rolling up astern of her.

The thrusting bow of the Yankee, Boston's candidate for the 1930 defense of the America's cup.

Shamrock V, the Nicholson-designed J class sloop which was the late Sir Thomas Lipton's last and finest vehicle for his assault against the America's cup. In the autumn of 1930 she met the American defender Enterprise and before the dimming eyes of the gallant "Tommy" suffered defeat.

Sending the ballooner up in stops. This cotton sail is secured with rottenstops (picturesquely but not too neatly in the present case) and with a man at the halliards to hoist away is hanked to the balloon jib stay. When the yacht frees her wind a strain is taken on the sheet, the stops part, and the big sail fills.

Long Island Sound Interclubs off before it. Since 1926 these Mower-designed 19-foot-waterline sloops have constituted the hottest class on the Sound, bringing to their helms many of the cleverest Corinthians of the East, racing weekly throughout the season, and never failing to provide close competition.

Nadji, a staysail schooner of the Seawan-
haka Corinthian class, lying over to it with
sheets eased on such a perfect day as
yachtsmen live for.

A ticklish moment for three of the New York Forties—Pampero on the port tack and Mistral holding the right of way, Shawara to leeward.

Airing, stopping, and bagging sail on deck of the Enterprise — or, as the news photographer quaintly phrased it at the time, "Putting stacks of canvas away in sacks, everybody happy, for they are the winning crew."

Breezing up. Rangoon, an An-
ker-designed 8-meter running in
a race on Long Island Sound.
With mainsail pressed hard
against the spreaders, two men
holding down the spinnaker
pole, and the tall Marconi mast
showing the pressure of the
wind, an owner's pleasure is
sometimes tinged with dread.

The Pinta, 42-foot transatlantic cruising racer, logged this day 56 miles in six hours. Toward the end of the period, the westerly continually freshening, the elastic limit of the spinnaker pole was almost reached.

Hotspur, a 26-foot-waterline cutter, bucking a hard easterly in a long distance race for cruising craft. Having aboard her a seasoned crew of ocean racing scoundrels she took it with jib topsail set—and liked it.

Where the rushing power of the wind, contested by straining canvas, is transmuted into clouds of flying spray. The cup defense candidate Weetamoe thrashing into it in one of her trials.

Highland Light, which, in 1932, covered the 628 miles between Montauk Point and Bermuda in two days, 23½ hours, is here caught under easy canvas in the rolling swells off the Fastnet.

The Pacific Ocean on a day when
there's not much to be done about it.

The famous yawl Dorade, only 37 feet on the waterline, but victor over vessels nearly twice her size in the 1931 transatlantic race to Plymouth. Designed by Olin Stephens, she was commanded and navigated by him in that 3,000-mile event and in the subsequent Fastnet race which she also tucked away.

The Istalena, a double-ended M boat.

Come, boys, put some beef into that.

Again the Enterprise, on an early trial before her metal mast was stepped or her Park Avenue boom shipped—in short, before she was in trim for her successful defense of the America's cup. Yet the picture, caught from an unconventional angle, is chock-full of technical interest.

There are times when Dorade
is thought to be a bit tender.

Aloft in the schooner Brilliant, Bermuda bound. The tufts of bagywrinkle on the shrouds were bent to prevent chafing of the sails against the wire when running free. There is, however, blessed little running on the Bermuda course. The elegantly mustachioed sailor on the cross-trees is not looking for his landfall on Bermuda.

Carlsark's owner was once advised by a tugboat skipper
to take his toy boat home and sail it in the bathtub.
Carlsark had that day returned from a voyage to Greece.

So perfectly proportioned is Resolute, Herreshoff's 1920 cup defender, that she seems at first glance to be another bathtub sailer. But there is a man 100 feet up her mast.

Atair, a New York Thirty, one of a Herreshoff class that has raced for nearly thirty years. They never reef.

A broad river of foam streaking out
astern of the schooner La Goleta.

Bow wave of the Wander Bird,
ex-pilot schooner which each
summer makes a European voyage with a crew of young amateur sailors. The heyday of the
square-rigged ship has passed,

but the small fore-and-after is coming into its own, every year finding more yachtsmen going foreign in the little wind ships. Above, semaphoring a passing steamer to report all well.

Rail well under and
sailing fast—Mistral,
New York Forty.

A knock-down drag-out for Victories and others. On such a day when there is a little more than a whole sail breeze nobody wants to reef unless the others do, so they sail with eased sheets, spilling some of the wind, but taking a beating in the puffs.

The opinion is entertained by some that all this is uncomfortable and hazardous—that the saddle of a bucking broncho is less uneasy than the sloping, slippery deck of a yacht. Yet the sailor waving from the Rowdy seems to be heartily enjoying himself.

The 12-meter Anitra, steady as a church despite the heaving groundswell.

Setting the ballooner of the Enchantress,
one of the big schooners of the San Pedro
fleet.

A stern chase is a long chase, and they'll
have to steal his wind if they want to over-
take him.

The last of the schooner Adriana. But
for the heroic intervention of Bobby
Somerset, British owner of the cutter
Jolie Brise, all her crew would have per-
ished in the dead of night.

The Brise herself, stunning pictorially
but not quite happy nautically. However, a cutter with her glowing interna-
tional reputation need not worry over
a parted spinnaker guy.

The Bagheera, running, as usual, for
shelter in a race on Lake Michigan.
The shelter lay just beyond the finish.

An illustration of what happens with an
eager ocean racing crew when the
mate calls for an extra hand forward.

The main boom of the Pinta
tripping in midocean.

Gulf Stream weather, the cook (recumbent)
dreaming "Death, where is thy sting?"

But if the piano may be brought out on deck
who wouldn't sell a farm and go to sea?

The master of the Water Gipsy, having just taken one green one down the back of his neck, stands up to ease it past his belt line, unworried by the next comber rambling up astern.

Balloon staysail, balloon jib,
spinnaker silently working a
thousand miles from land. At
daybreak a member of the
watch takes a look around,
happy to be a racing salt

STAND BY! STORM WARNING FLYING

New York Forties in a
squall off Larchmont.

The Sally Ann off Newport—
bow lifting, scud flying, smoky
sou'wester brewing.

The Interclub Blue Streak after she had
jibed and carried away her shrouds,
but before her mast let go. It blew a
45-mile gale that day and she was
not the only boat to notice it.

There was no collision. The schooner Venturer sailed by just as the New York Forty Marilee jibed and carried away her topmast.

After a man overboard had been rescued the Marilee, a trifle haywire, awaited a line from a motor boat and was towed to port.

Again they did not come together. It is moments like this, however, that give joy to the photographer and arouse no great concern in the yachtsmen involved.

With two reefs down and all hands sitting pretty, the cutter Water Witch slides down the back of a Farralone Islands graybeard. Here's looking at you, sailors.

It's not so bad when you're dressed for i

A moment or two after a puff caught the M boat Valiant wrong and shivered her experimental duralumin mast.

To make matters worse the mast stuck in the mud and stayed there until a wrecking barge was requisitioned.

Not the perfect end of a perfect day—a Sonder boat sinking
in the Sound

And not the preferred method
of lowering sail when picking up
a mooring.

With sails no longer crowding
the fleet comes home to rest.

Good luck, sailor.
Big sheaves and
small ropes to you.

INDEX OF PHOTOGRAPHERS

Morris Rosenfeld   Golliwogg; Quest; Thistle; Malabar X; Long Island Sound Interclubs; Nadji; Rangoon; Hotspur; Weetamoe (copyright by Rosenfeld); Istalena; Enterprise (stern view); Dorade (deck view); Resolute (copyright by Rosenfeld); A knock-down dragout; Rowdy; Anitra (copyright by Rosenfeld); Interclub losing her mast; Valiant; Uncaptioned sunrise.

Edwin Levick   Six-meters starting; Pleione; Larchmont week; Vanitie; Enterprise (view from aloft); Migrant; Yankee; Shamrock V; Forties meeting; Atair; Mistral; Forties in a squall; Sally Ann; Venturer and Marilee; Marilee; Sonder boat sinking.

Ellsworth Ford   Frostbiting; Seven Bells; Brilliant; Stern chase; Daybreak at sea; Good luck, sailor; Tailpiece (buoy).

Alfred F. Loomis   Atlantic; Aloft in Atlantic; Pinta (spinnaker pole bending); La Goleta; Lending a hand forward; Pinta (main boom tripping); Gulf Stream weather; "Who wouldn't sell a farm?"

W. C. Sawyer   Sending the ballooner up; Pacific Ocean calm; Hands on the main sheet.

Ray Chapin   Star boats; Wiletie; Enchantress; Again they didn't come together.

Beken & Son   Six-meters in the Solent; Nina; Jolie Brise.

Irving Johnson   Wander Bird; Adriana burning.

Rotofotos   Mother Goose; "It's not so bad."

Ernest Tanare   Atlantics ramming committee boat; Dinghies on landing float.

Acme News   Enterprise (airing sail); Water Witch.

C. H. J. Snider   Toronto trophy race; Mainsail splitting.

F. W. Tupper   Inland Lakes scow; Storm warning.

A. P. Butler   Water Gipsy; Highland Light.

Nesmith-Ford   Dorade (outboard view).

Nesmith-Blackington—Squalls pass and the sun shines.

H. R. Hollyday   Flying Cloud.

Troy   Carlsark.

Keystone View   Elaine.

Porter Varney   Twenty-one foot Fish class sloops.

Robert C. Herrmann—Bagheera.

(The uncaptioned photographs accompanying the foreword were taken by the following photographers: Ellsworth Ford, W. C. Sawyer, Morris Rosenfeld, Fred Bradley, Edwin Levick, Godknows, W. C. Sawyer, Rotofotos, Fred Bradley, and W. C. Sawyer.)